Five-Minute
SUNDAY SCHOOL
ACTIVITIES

MW00526368

Built On A Rock

For information regarding the CPSIA on this printed material call:
203-595-3636 and provide reference # LANC-538867

rainbowpublishers®
www.RainbowPublishers.com

Rainbow Publishers • P.O. Box 261129 • San Diego, CA 92196

Five-Minute
SUNDAY SCHOOL ACTIVITIES

Built On A Rock

Karen Wingate

To Dr. Eleanor Daniel, who has invested her life in teaching reliable men and women so that they may teach others (2 Timothy 2:2).

FIVE-MINUTE SUNDAY SCHOOL ACTIVITIES: BUILT ON A ROCK
©2014 by Rainbow Publishers, second printing
ISBN 10: 1-58411-099-6
ISBN 13: 978-1-58411-099-6
Rainbow reorder# RB38423
RELIGION / Christian Ministry / Children

Rainbow Publishers
P.O. Box 261129
San Diego, CA 92196
www.RainbowPublishers.com

Interior Illustrator: Chuck Galey
Cover Illustrator: Brie Spangler

Scriptures are from the *Holy Bible: New International Version* (North American Edition), ©1973, 1978, 1984 by the International Bible Society. Used by permission of Zondervan Bible Publishers.

Printed in the United States of America

Contents

Introduction

The church is an exciting, vibrant group of people that God uses to spread the news of His plan for our salvation through His Son. This book is all about how God built His church, according to the biblical account found in the book of Acts. The activities and stories here are designed to help your children walk in the footsteps of those early Christians and inspire them to share the exciting news about Jesus with others.

Five-Minute Sunday School Activities is designed to give teachers a quick activity that teaches an important Bible truth. Teachers are often faced with a few extra minutes after the lesson is finished. There are also times when a teacher needs a few moments to get attendance and other important matters out of the way before the main lesson. Instead of wasting these minutes with non-learning play, provide a *Five-Minute Sunday School Activity*!

The activities in this book can also be used as entire lessons. Bible story references, teaching suggestions, and memory verses are included with each activity.

Extra Time suggestions are given for each activity. If you have more than five minutes, extend the lesson time with the **Extra Time** option.

Who is Jesus?
MATTHEW 16:13-19

✓ **MEMORY VERSE**

Simon Peter answered, "You are the Christ, the Son of the living God."
~ Matthew 16:16

WHAT YOU NEED

- page 10, duplicated
- markers
- pencils

BEFORE CLASS

Duplicate a pattern page for each child.

WHAT TO DO

1. Introduce the lesson by asking, **What is a church? Who is Jesus?** Tell the story from Matthew 16:13-19. Say, **Many people thought Jesus was a prophet or a great teacher sent from God. Peter said Jesus was the Son of God.**
2. Distribute a pattern page to each child. Read the memory verse.
3. Ask children to draw a church above the memory verse rock. Read Matthew 16:18. Say, **A church is a group of people who get together because they all believe Jesus is the Son of God. Everything they do together is built on what they believe about Jesus.**
4. Ask the children to autograph each other's papers inside the church drawings. Say, **All of us are together today because we believe Jesus is the Son of God.**

EXTRA TIME

Play a "Who Am I?" game. Children will take turns naming names of famous people such as a President, a teacher, or the minister at your church. They will then ask, "Who Am I?" The other children will tell who that person is. Several times during the game, ask "Who is Jesus?" The children should all shout, "He is the Son of God!"

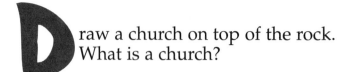

Draw a church on top of the rock.
What is a church?

SIMON PETER ANSWERED, "YOU ARE THE
CHRIST, THE SON OF THE LIVING GOD."

MATTHEW 16:16

The Disciples Tell About Jesus
MATTHEW 10:1-10, LUKE 10:1-4, 17-24

✓ MEMORY VERSE

As you go, preach this message:
"The kingdom of heaven is near."
~ Matthew 10:7

WHAT YOU NEED

- page 12, duplicated
- pencils
- crayons

BEFORE CLASS

Duplicate a pattern page for each child.

WHAT TO DO

1. Introduce the lesson by telling the story from Matthew 10:1-10 and Luke 10:1-4, 17-24. Ask, **How many men did Jesus send out the first time? How many men did He send the second time? What did Jesus tell them to do?**
2. Distribute a pattern page to each child.
3. Read the memory verse.
4. Tell the children to write the names of the twelve disciples in the right blanks, using the word box on the side of the page. Say, **Jesus taught his disciples to do the same things He was doing so they could tell other people the Good News about Him**. As time allows, let students color the pictures of the disciples.

EXTRA TIME

Challenge the children to memorize the names of the twelve disciples. Have them create a chant of the twelve names to help them remember.

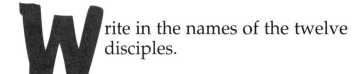rite in the names of the twelve disciples.

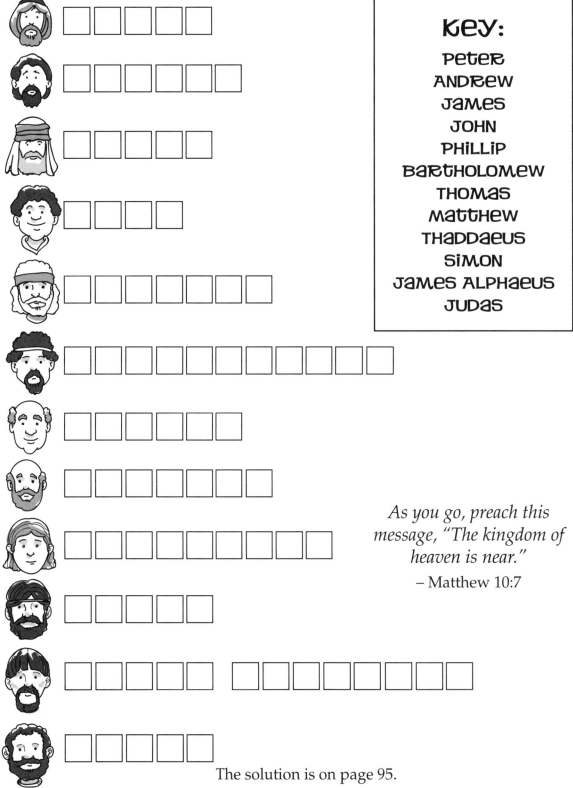

KEY:

PETER
ANDREW
JAMES
JOHN
PHILLIP
BARTHOLOMEW
THOMAS
MATTHEW
THADDAEUS
SIMON
JAMES ALPHAEUS
JUDAS

As you go, preach this message, "The kingdom of heaven is near."
– Matthew 10:7

The solution is on page 95.

...us is Arrested
?K 14:43-50, 53, 55-64

...RY VERSE

*...on of Man must suffer many
...he must be killed and on the
third day be raised to life."*
~ Luke 9:22

YOU NEED

...1, duplicated

...s

...E CLASS

...a pattern page for each child. On a sample page, fill in the speech bubbles
...you the Christ, the Son of the Blessed One?" and, "I am."

...TO DO

...oduce the lesson by telling the story from Mark 14:43-50, 53, 55-64. Say, **Of
...people, the leaders should have known that Jesus was God's Son.
...tead, they arrested Jesus and decided to kill Him, even though He did
...hing wrong.**
...tribute a pattern page to each child.
...ad the memory verse. Say, **Jesus knew the leaders would arrest him and
...t him to death. He knew this because He was God's Son.**
...ad Mark 14:61,62. Show your sample pattern page to the children. Ask,
...hat did the chief priest say? What did Jesus say? Have the children write
...hat each said in the appropriate speech bubble. When they finish, they may
...lor the page. Say, **The leaders thought it was a crime to claim to be God's
...on. But Jesus really was God's Son.**

EXTRA TIME

Make a graffiti board. Have the children write or draw on a poster board or white
board about a time when they have been treated or punished unfairly. Say, **Jesus
knows how you feel because He was unfairly treated too. But He did not fight the
people who arrested Him.**

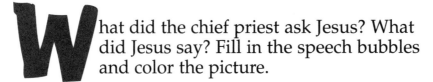

What did the chief priest ask Jesus? What did Jesus say? Fill in the speech bubbles and color the picture.

And He said, "The Son of Man must suffer many things and be rejected by the elders, chief priests and teachers of the law, and he must be killed and on the third day be raised to life."
– Luke 9:22

The solution is on page 95.

Peter Denies Jesus
MARK 14:27-31, 54, 66-72

✓MEMORY VERSE

Whoever acknowledges me before men, I will also acknowledge him before my Father in heaven.
~ Matthew 10:32

WHAT YOU NEED

- page 16, duplicated
- scissors
- tape
- markers or crayons

BEFORE CLASS

Duplicate a pattern page for each child. Make a sample craft to show the children.

WHAT TO DO

1. Introduce the lesson by telling the story from Mark 14:27-31, 54, 66-72. As you tell the story, have children keep track on their fingers how many times Peter denied he knew Jesus, telling the children to crow like a rooster when they reach three times. Ask, **Why do you think Peter said he didn't know Jesus?**
2. Show the sample craft to the children.
3. Distribute a pattern page to each child.
4. Say the memory verse.
5. Have children color and cut apart the pictures and place them in chronological order according to the story. Ask, **How would you feel if your best friend were afraid to admit he knew you?** Say, **Peter was afraid the soldiers would arrest him, too. Because Jesus is the Son of God, we don't have to be afraid of what could happen to us. Jesus wants us to be willing to admit we know Him and follow Him.**

EXTRA TIME

Lead a cheer for Jesus. Divide the group into two teams. Have them face each other. Have the two groups call back and forth to each other, "I know Jesus/Yes I do/I know Jesus/How 'bout you?" On the word "you" the team leading the cheer points to the other team, who repeats the cheer, pointing back to the first team.

Put the pictures in the right order. Color the story strip. Tell the story to a friend.

Whoever acknowledges me before men, I will also acknowledge him before my Father in heaven.
– Matthew 10:32

The solution is on page 95.

Jesus is Crucified
MARK 15

✓ MEMORY VERSE

*Greater love has no one than this,
that he lay down his life for his friends.*
~ John 15:13

WHAT YOU NEED

- page 18, duplicated on card stock
- glitter, small beans or yarn
- glue

BEFORE CLASS

Duplicate a pattern page for each child. Make a sample craft to show the children.

WHAT TO DO

1. Introduce the lesson by telling the story from Mark 15. Ask, **How did Jesus die?** Say, **This was a terrible, painful, and embarrassing way for Him to die. Jesus could have rescued Himself. He didn't have to let those bad men kill Him.**
2. Show the sample craft to the children.
3. Distribute a pattern page to each child.
4. Say the memory verse. Ask, **Who did Jesus die for? Why did He die for you and me?**
5. Have the children trace the letters with glue then with glitter, small beans, yarn, or an art medium of your choice. Say, **Jesus didn't do anything wrong so He didn't deserve to die. Instead, He decided to take the punishment all of us deserve for all the wrong things we have done. He did it because He loves us.**

EXTRA TIME

Print each word of the memory verse on a separate index card. Shuffle the cards and have the children place the cards in the right order in the shape of a cross. Reshuffle the cards, this time having the children place the cards in the shape of a heart.

Five Minute

Trace the letters with glue, then with glitter, beans, or pieces of yarn. Why did Jesus die for you?

Greater love has no one than this, that he lay down his life for his friends.
– John 15:13

Jesus is Alive
JOHN 20:1-20

✓ MEMORY VERSE

But God raised him from the dead, freeing him from the agony of death, because it was impossible for death to keep its hold on him.
~ Acts 2:24

WHAT YOU NEED

- page 20, duplicated
- scissors
- reusable adhesive
- crayons

BEFORE CLASS

Duplicate a pattern page for each child. Make a sample craft to show the children.

WHAT TO DO

1. Introduce the lesson by telling the story from John 20:1-20. Ask, **Who went to Jesus' grave? What did she find? Who spoke to her? What happened to Jesus?**
2. Show the sample craft to the children.
3. Distribute a pattern page to each child.
4. Say the memory verse. Say, **Jesus was God's Son. The Bible says it was impossible for Jesus to stay dead.**
5. Have the children first color the tomb and the figures, then cut them out. Have them fold the picture of Jesus and Mary on the dotted lines and fold the tomb so only the blocked passage is showing. Then have them unfold the tomb to reveal the opening where Jesus emerged. Ask each child to tell the story using their cut-outs. Say, **Jesus really did die. But He had the power to come back to life because He was God's Son.**

EXTRA TIME

Have the children form the words, "Jesus Is Alive," using Easter basket grass. Place a large sheet of paper on your table surface or on the floor so they keep the grass on the paper.

ake a story scene. Color the picture. Fold back the picture of Jesus. Cut out the stone. Where was the stone when Mary came to the tomb?

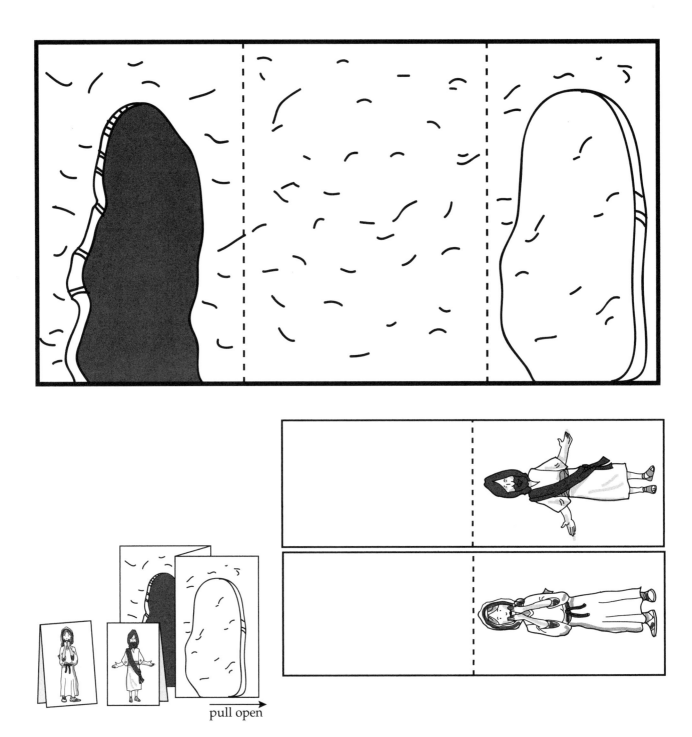

pull open

But God raised him from the dead, freeing him from the agony of death, because it was impossible for death to keep its hold on him.
– Acts 2:24

Jesus and Thomas
JOHN 20:19-29

✓ MEMORY VERSE

Thomas said to him, "My Lord and my God!"
~ John 20:28

WHAT YOU NEED

- page 22, duplicated
- Bibles
- ⅜ inch adhesive bandages
- red markers
- crayons

BEFORE CLASS

Duplicate a pattern page for each child. Make a sample craft to show the children.

WHAT TO DO

1. Introduce the lesson by telling the story from John 20:19-29. Say, **Thomas didn't believe that Jesus was alive. He wanted to see Jesus for himself before he believed.**
2. Show the sample craft to the children.
3. Distribute a pattern page to each child.
4. Help children find John 20:28 in the Bibles. Read the verse together. Direct them to fill in the missing words on their pattern page.
5. Tell the children to put an adhesive bandage on Jesus' side and use the red markers to show the nail wounds in His wrists. Say, **Thomas had to see Jesus before he could believe Jesus was alive. We can believe Jesus is alive even though we've never seen Him because the Bible tells us so.**

EXTRA TIME

Play a game of Seven-Up. Choose up to seven volunteers. Have the rest of the children sit in a circle with their heads down and their thumbs raised. The volunteers will each touch one person's thumb. The children will try to guess who touched their thumb. Say, **You didn't see who touched you but you believed that person was in the room. We can believe Jesus came back to life even though we don't get to see Him like Thomas did.**

Five Minute

olor the picture. Draw the nail wounds in Jesus' wrists. Put an adhesive bandage on Jesus' side. Fill in the missing words in the memory verse.

Thomas said to him,

"My _ _ _ _

and my _ _ _ !"

– John 20:28

Jesus Fixes Breakfast
JOHN 21:1-14

✓ MEMORY VERSE

None of the disciples dared ask Him, "Who are You?" They knew it was the Lord.
~ John 21:12

WHAT YOU NEED

- page 24, duplicated
- scissors
- glue sticks

BEFORE CLASS

Duplicate a pattern page for each child. Make a sample game to show the children.

WHAT TO DO

1. Introduce the lesson by telling the story from John 21:1-14. Say, **Once before, Jesus helped His disciples catch a big bunch of fish. Helping them catch a miraculous amount of fish this time showed the disciples it really was Jesus who was alive again.**
2. Show the game to the children.
3. Distribute a pattern page to each child.
4. Say the memory verse. Ask, **How did the disciples know this man was Jesus?**
5. Help the children cut out the questions and answers and match each question to the correct answer, gluing them back to back.
6. Pair up the children. Have them combine their two sets of questions and take turns reading a question to their partner who will answer it. Say, **Only Jesus could make that big catch of fish happen. This man on the beach had to be Jesus who had come back to life!**

EXTRA TIME

Have the children count out 153 fish crackers and divide them among themselves. Have them place their crackers in berry baskets or netting. Say, **Jesus showed the disciples He had come back to life by helping them catch a miraculous amount of fish.**

ut out the questions and answers. Glue the correct answer to the back of each question. Play a game with a friend.

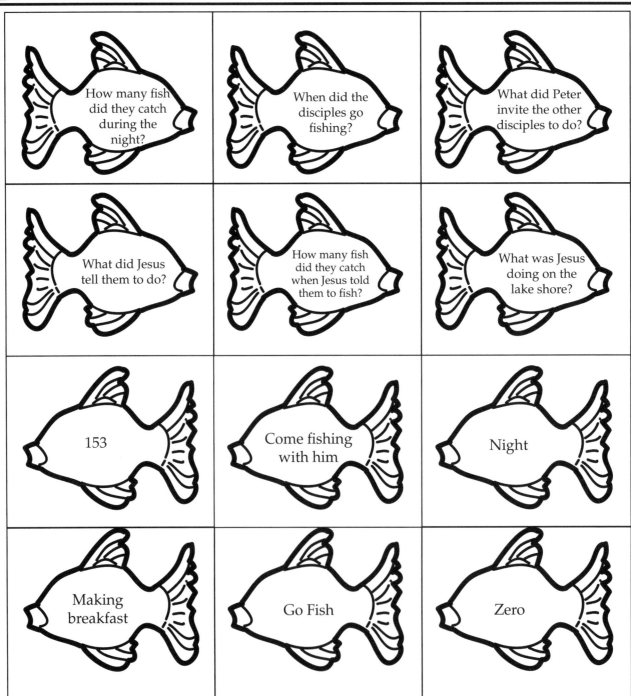

How many fish did they catch during the night?

When did the disciples go fishing?

What did Peter invite the other disciples to do?

What did Jesus tell them to do?

How many fish did they catch when Jesus told them to fish?

What was Jesus doing on the lake shore?

153

Come fishing with him

Night

Making breakfast

Go Fish

Zero

None of the disciples dared ask Him, "Who are You?"
They knew it was the Lord.
– John 21:12

The solution is on page 95.

Jesus Gives His Followers a Job to Do
MATTHEW 28:16-20, LUKE 24:36-49

✓ MEMORY VERSE

You will be my witnesses in Jerusalem, and in all Judea and Samaria, and to the ends of the earth.
~ Acts 1:8

WHAT YOU NEED

- page 26, duplicated
- pencils
- colored pencils

BEFORE CLASS

Duplicate a pattern page for each child. Make a sample craft to show the children.

WHAT TO DO

1. Introduce the lesson by telling the story from Matthew 28:16-20, Luke 24:36-49. Say, **A witness is someone who has seen something happen and tells others about it. The disciples were witnesses of Jesus' miracles, His death, and how He came back to life. Jesus wanted them to tell other people about all the things He had done.**
2. Distribute a pattern page to each child and say the memory verse together.
3. Show the sample craft to the children. Ask, **If Jesus gave this job to us, where would He want us to tell people about Him?** Say, **Let's change our verse to show all the places Jesus wants us to go to.**
4. Have students write their names and draw a picture of themselves at the top of the page. Help students spell the name of the city and state where they live and the name of one of the adjoining states. Have each student think of a foreign country. Help them write that country next to the arrow at the bottom of the page. Have students read their personalized paraphrase of the verse.

EXTRA TIME

Have volunteers locate their home town, state and other near by states on a globe. Spin the globe, stop, and have a child blindly touch a spot on the globe. Say, **You can pray that people in this country learn about Jesus. Someday, God may even use you to tell people in that country about Jesus.**

f Jesus were talking to you, where would He want you to be a witness? Fill in the memory verse with the places where you live.

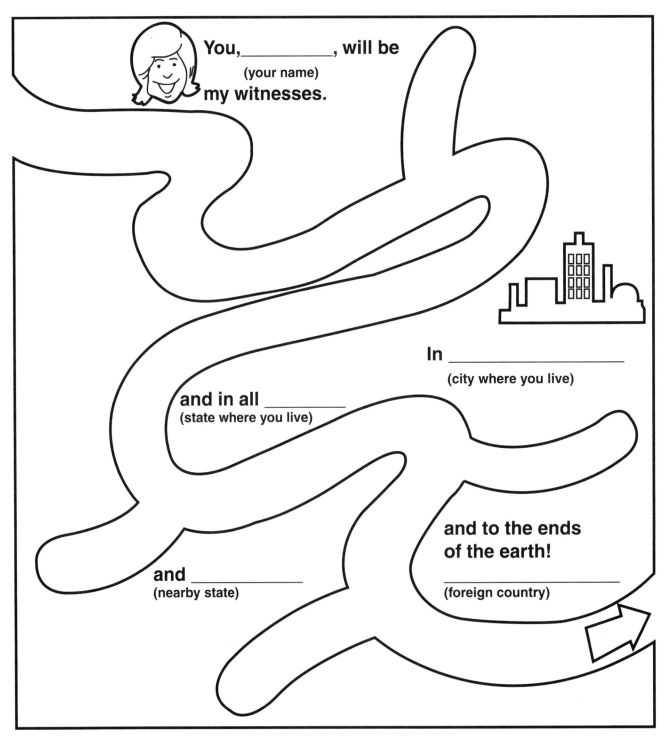

You,_____, will be
(your name)
my witnesses.

In _____
(city where you live)

and in all _____
(state where you live)

and _____
(nearby state)

and to the ends
of the earth!
_____
(foreign country)

You will be my witnesses in Jerusalem and in all Judea, and Samaria and to the ends of the earth.
– Acts 1:8

Jesus Returns to Heaven
LUKE 24:50-53, MARK 16:19, ACTS 1:9-11

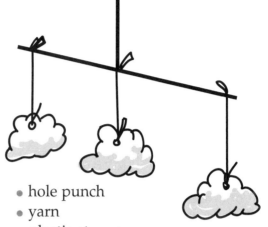

✓ MEMORY VERSE

This same Jesus, who has been taken from you into heaven, will come back in the same way you have seen him go into heaven.
~ Acts 1:11

WHAT YOU NEED

- page 28, duplicated on card stock
- scissors
- cotton balls
- glue
- hole punch
- yarn
- plastic straws

BEFORE CLASS

Duplicate a pattern page for each child. Make a sample craft to show the children.

WHAT TO DO

1. Introduce the lesson by telling the story from Luke 24:50-53, Mark 16:19 and Acts 1:9-11. Ask, **Where did Jesus go? Will people on earth ever see Jesus again?**
2. Show the sample craft to the children.
3. Distribute a pattern page to each child. Say the memory verse.
4. Direct children to make a mobile. They will cut out the clouds, glue cotton balls around the edges, punch a hole in the top, and tie a piece of yarn to each cloud. Help children tie a loop in the other end of the yarn and insert a plastic straw through the loops to make a mobile.
5. Say, **Jesus' work on earth was done. He got to go back to heaven to live and reign with God, His Father. He promised to come back someday. If we believe in Him, He will take us to heaven to live with Him.**

EXTRA TIME

Have the children make a diorama of Heaven's throne room. Using an open shoe box, glue gold foil paper to the bottom and sides. Make two thrones with small craft sticks and gold foil. Have children label one throne, "GOD" and the throne to the right, "JESUS." Say, **When Jesus went to heaven, He was no longer a man. He had a heavenly body. He now could reign in heaven with God.**

Make a mobile to remind you that Jesus is coming back someday!

Jesus went to heaven.

Jesus reigns in heaven with God.

Jesus is coming back someday.

This same Jesus, who has been taken from you into heaven,
will come back in the same way you have seen him go into heaven.
– Acts 1:11

God Starts the Church
ACTS 2:1-12, 22-24, 36-41

✓ MEMORY VERSE

Therefore, let all Israel be assured of this: God has made this Jesus, whom you crucified, both Lord and Christ.

~ Acts 2:36

WHAT YOU NEED

- page 30, duplicated

BEFORE CLASS

Duplicate a pattern page for each child.

WHAT TO DO

1. Introduce the lesson by telling the story from Acts 2:1-12, 22-24, 36-41. Say, **God sent the wind and the fire and gave the disciples the ability to speak in different languages. He did this so all the people would know that God had decided it was time to start the church.**
2. Distribute a pattern page to each child.
3. Say the memory verse with the children. Say, **Peter wanted everyone to know that the man they knew as Jesus really was the Son of God. People who belong to God's church believe that Jesus is God's Son.**
4. Review the motions on the pattern page with the children. Divide them into small groups to practice saying the story and doing the motions.
5. Repeat the memory verse together. Ask, **What makes the church special? What special thing about Jesus do people in the church believe?**

EXTRA TIME

Practice the "Story In Motion" with the entire group. Arrange to perform it for another class, a children's worship service or for your adult worship.

ct out the story with your friends. Have someone recite the words while everyone else performs.

 **Wind blew.**

 Fire fell.

 The crowd listened.

 Peter spoke,
"You crucified Jesus."

 **The crowd cried out,**
"What do we do?"

 **The disciples preached,**
"Come to Jesus."

 3000 came.

 **The church began.**

Therefore, let all Israel be assured of this:
God has made this Jesus, whom you
crucified, both Lord and Christ.
– Acts 2:36

30

The Church Gets Busy
ACTS 2:42-47

✓ MEMORY VERSE

They devoted themselves to the apostles' teaching and to fellowship, to the breaking of bread and to prayer.
~ Acts 2:42

WHAT YOU NEED

- page 32, duplicated
- crayons

BEFORE CLASS

Duplicate a pattern page for each child.

WHAT TO DO

1. Ask, **What things do people do at church?** Describe what the beginning church did as found in Acts 2:42-47. Say, **When the church first started, the people were excited. They liked spending time together. They wanted to learn more about Jesus. They wanted to praise God for doing such wonderful things for them.**
2. Distribute a pattern page and crayons to each child.
3. Read the memory verse.
4. Direct the children to circle the scenes that show activities of the early church as you read. Read Acts 2:42-47. The children should circle only six different scenes. Ask, **How are these activities similar to what we do in church today?** As time allows, let children color the coloring page.

EXTRA TIME

Help your group plan a worship service, trying to include as many of the activities of the early church as they can. Plan a time when your group can lead your worship service for other children or for the parents of the children in your class.

ircle and label six scenes of what people in the new church did. Not all of the scenes should be circled.

They devoted themselves to the apostles'
teaching and to fellowship.
to the breaking of bread and to prayer.
– Acts 2:42

The solution is on page 95.

Peter and John Speak Up for Jesus
ACTS 4:1-22

✓ MEMORY VERSE

When they saw the courage of Peter and John and realized that they were unschooled, ordinary men, they were astonished and they took note that these men had been with Jesus.
~ Acts 4:13

WHAT YOU NEED

- page 34, duplicated
- crayons or markers
- scissors
- tape

BEFORE CLASS

Duplicate a pattern page for each child. Make a sample craft to show the children.

WHAT TO DO

1. Introduce the lesson by telling the story from Acts 4:1-22. Say, **Before they met Jesus, Peter and John caught fish for a living. They were not famous or important. Yet they were willing to talk about Jesus to these important leaders!**
2. Distribute a pattern page to each child.
3. Read the memory verse together.
4. Have the children color the pictures of Peter and John. Have them cut out the two puppets, taping the edges together to make finger puppets. Have them use the puppets to tell the story.
5. Ask, **Who can God use to tell other people about Jesus?** Say, **God can use ordinary people like you and me to tell people about Jesus.** Have the children draw a picture of themselves on one puppet and a picture of someone they know on the other puppet.

EXTRA TIME

Have the children use the drawn puppets of themselves and someone they know to role play talking to someone about Jesus.

Use finger puppets to show who God uses to talk about Jesus. Draw yourself and a friend in the blank boxes then cut out each finger puppet.

Peter	When they saw the courage of Peter and John and realized that they were unschooled, ordinary men, they were astonished and they took note that these men had been with Jesus. — *Acts 4:13*
John	When they saw the courage of Peter and John and realized that they were unschooled, ordinary men, they were astonished and they took note that these men had been with Jesus. — *Acts 4:13*

The Believers Share Their Possessions
ACTS 4:32-37

✓ MEMORY VERSE

They shared everything they had.
~ Acts 4:32

WHAT YOU NEED

- page 36, duplicated
- Bibles
- pencils
- crayons

BEFORE CLASS

Duplicate a pattern page for each child.

WHAT TO DO

1. Introduce the lesson by reading the text from Acts 4:32-37. Say, **The new church took care of people who had needs. They treated each other like family!**
2. Distribute a pattern page to each child. Ask, **What kinds of things do you think the people shared with each other?**
3. Distribute Bibles. Help children locate Acts 4:32. Direct them to write the words of the memory verse in order, using the Bibles as needed. Have them draw a picture of something they can share with a needy person. As time allows, let them color the rest of the page.
4. Repeat the memory verse together.

EXTRA TIME

Have children work together to decorate several wicker baskets, using gift wrap, felt, or fabric. Ask the children to bring in extra school supplies from home (crayons, pencils, paper, folders, glue sticks, and so forth) to your next session. Plan to give the baskets to a needy family with school age children.

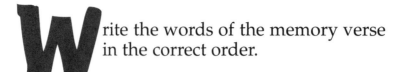

W rite the words of the memory verse in the correct order.

_____ _____ _____ _____ _____.

– Acts 4:32

Draw a picture of something you own that you can share with someone.

The solution is on page 95.

Ananias and Sapphira Cheat God

ACTS 5:1-11

✓ MEMORY VERSE

Do not lie to each other, since you have taken off your old self with its practices.
~ Colossians 3:9

WHAT YOU NEED

- page 38, duplicated
- pencils

BEFORE CLASS

Duplicate a pattern page for each child.

WHAT TO DO

1. Introduce the lesson by telling the story from Acts 5:1-11. Ask, **Were Ananias and Sapphira wrong to give money to the apostles? Were they wrong to keep money for themselves?** Say, **Ananias and Sapphira were not honest. They gave the impression that they were giving all the money from the sale of their land. They were lying to make themselves look good.**
2. Distribute a pattern page to each child.
3. Have children complete the verse, using the code on the pattern page. Say, **God is very serious when He tells us He doesn't want us to lie to each other.**
4. Have the children read the memory verse together. Talk about things that children are tempted to lie about.

EXTRA TIME

Have the children act out alternate endings to the story of Ananias and Sapphira. Alternate endings could include the couple giving all the money from the sale, giving only part of the money and saying so to the apostles, or quietly putting money in an offering plate without telling anyone where the money came from.

se the code below to solve the
memory verse puzzle.

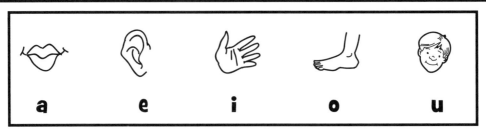

| a | e | i | o | u |

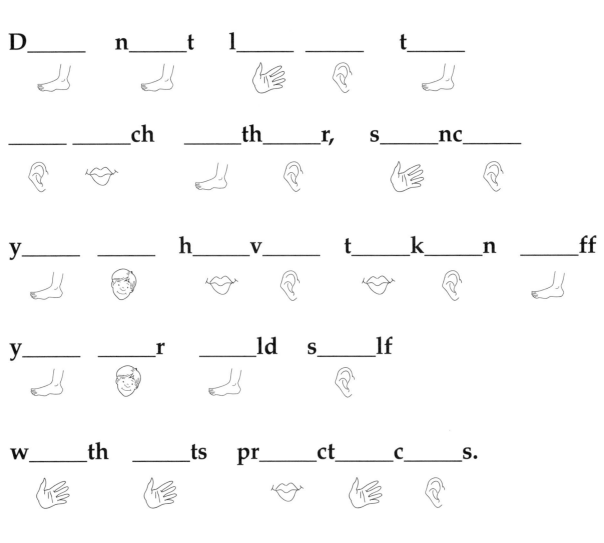

D____ n____t l____ ____ t____

____ ____ch ____th____r, s____nc____

y____ ____ h____v____ t____k____n ____ff

y____ ____r ____ld s____lf

w____th ____ts pr____ct____c____s.

– C____l____ss ____ ____ ns 3:9

The solution is on page 95.

Barnabas Encourages the Church
ACTS 4:36,37; 9:26-31; 11:19-30

✓ MEMORY VERSE

But encourage one another daily, as long as it is called Today, so that none of you may be hardened by sin's deceitfulness.
~ Hebrews 3:13

WHAT YOU NEED

- page 40, duplicated
- crayons

BEFORE CLASS

Duplicate a pattern page for each child. Color a sample page, drawing pictures of yourself in each of the current day pictures.

WHAT TO DO

1. Say, **There is a man in the Bible who was an encourager. An encourager is like a cheerleader or a helper. When you hear something this man did that was encouraging, raise your hand.** Tell the three separate incidents about Barnabas from Acts 4:36,37; 9:26-31; 11:19-30. Say, **Barnabas was an encourager to people in the new church, especially to a man named Saul.**
2. Show the sample page. Say, **You and I can be encouragers too.**
3. Distribute a pattern page to each child. Say the memory verse together.
4. Have children take turns reading the three ways Barnabas was an encourager. Have children write their names and draw a picture of themselves in each of the three right hand pictures. Ask, **What other ways can you encourage your friends?**

EXTRA TIME

Play a relay race. Divide children into two teams. Mark a start and finish line. Have children take turns running to the finish line and back, touching the next person while the rest of the team cheers on each runner. The team who wins is not the team who finishes first but the team who is the most encouraging.

Barnabas encouraged others. You can too! Write your name on the blank lines and draw yourself inside the encouraging child in the pictures on the right side. Color the pictures.

BARNABAS

ME

Barnabas gave money to help the church.

_____ can give money to help the church grow.

Barnabas helped Saul join the other Christians.

_____ can help someone join my group.

Barnabas worked with Saul to start a church.   _____ can invite someone to work with me for Jesus.

But encourage one another daily, as long as it is called Today,
so that none of you may be hardened by sin's deceitfulness.
– Hebrews 3:13

Seven Men Help the Church
ACTS 6:1-7

✓ MEMORY VERSE

If anyone serves, he should do it with the strength God provides, so that in all things, God may be praised through Jesus Christ.
~ 1 Peter 4:11

WHAT YOU NEED

- page 42, duplicated
- card stock
- pencils
- crayons
- glue sticks

BEFORE CLASS

Duplicate a pattern page for each child. Make a sample craft to show the children.

WHAT TO DO

1. Introduce the lesson by telling the story from Acts 6:1-7. Say, **The new church had a problem. They wanted to help the widows have enough to eat, but some ladies were being skipped over. They solved the problem by choosing seven men to help the church. Our church also has helpers that help the church take care of people.**
2. Show the sample craft to the children.
3. Distribute a pattern page to each child. Say the memory verse together.
4. Direct children to write on the figures the names of people who serve in your church in the following capacities: preacher, children's teacher, custodian, music leader, and greeter/usher. They will color and cut out the figures, gluing them on card stock or poster board to make stand up figures.
5. Read the memory verse again. Say, **God wants helpers in the church who love God and want to serve His way. The apostles chose seven men who loved and obeyed God.**

EXTRA TIME

Have the children write thank you notes to several of your church helpers. Have them include, under their signature, the reference to today's memory verse.

Who are the helpers in your church? Write their names on the figures below. Cut out the stand up figures. Put them where you can remember to pray for them.

If anyone serves, he should do it with the strength God provides, so that in all things, God may be praised through Jesus Christ.

– 1 Peter 4:11

Stephen Dies for His Faith in Jesus
ACTS 6:8-15; 7:1-60

✓ MEMORY VERSE

Be faithful, even to the point of death, and I will give you the crown of life.
~ Revelation 2:10

WHAT YOU NEED

- page 44, duplicated
- pencils

BEFORE CLASS

Duplicate a pattern page for each child.

WHAT TO DO

1. Introduce the lesson by telling the story from Acts 6:8-15; 7:1-60. Don't go into detail about Stephen's speech to the council; just tell the children that Stephen told the council about Jesus. Say, **Stephen told the council about his faith in Jesus. It made them so mad, they killed him. Stephen was willing to talk about Jesus even though he knew the people wouldn't like what he said.**
2. Distribute a pattern page to each child.
3. Say the memory verse. Say, **Maybe you won't die because you believe in Jesus. But you might lose friends or people might make fun of you. Jesus wants us to stay faithful to him no matter what happens because His way is the truth!**
4. Talk about the different situations on the pattern page. Ask, **What other times do we need to be faithful no matter if it's unpleasant?** Brainstorm ideas, then have the children write a way they will try to be faithful to God in the coming week.

EXTRA TIME

Teach the children the following words to the tune of "Row Row Row Your Boat:"
"Lord I want to be/fa-aith-ful and true/No matter what happens to me/I will follow you."

How will you stay faithful to God?

A family is gathered at the dinner table. You ask, "Can I pray before we start eating?"

In a classroom the teacher says, "Let's sing a Christmas song." You ask, "Can we sing a song about Baby Jesus?"

The coach says, "Be here for Sunday's game." You explain to him, "I can't. I go to church."

Write your own idea on the lines below.

_____

_____

_____

_____

_____

_____

Be faithful, even to the point of death, and I will give you the crown of life.
– Revelation 2:10

Philip and the Treasurer
ACTS 8:26-40

✓ MEMORY VERSE

Then Philip began with that very passage of Scripture and told him the good news about Jesus.
~ Acts 8:35

WHAT YOU NEED

- page 46, duplicated
- pencils

BEFORE CLASS

Duplicate a pattern page for each child.

WHAT TO DO

1. Introduce the lesson by telling the story from Acts 8:26-40. Ask, **Who did Philip meet? What was the important man doing? What did Philip do? How did the man react?** Say, **Philip met this man while he was traveling. He told the man about Jesus. We see people everyday, too. We can tell anyone we meet today about Jesus.**
2. Distribute a pattern page to each child.
3. Ask children to find the words of the memory verse by following the maze, writing the words in order on the lines below.
4. Ask children to write names of people they come in contact with everyday, such as friends, teachers, family members, neighbors, and store clerks. Ask, **How can you talk about Jesus to these people?**
5. Repeat the memory verse together.

EXTRA TIME

Play a variation of "Hang Man" with the children. As words to guess, use the types of people children see everyday such as a teacher, or a leader in the church. Have a child privately tell you his or her chosen word, then write the blanks on a board. Correctly guessed letters go on the line. If kids guess letters that aren't in the word, the player can draw the parts of a chariot (wagon) for each missed letter. The first person to guess the word may be the next player

Who are people you see everyday? Write their names on the lines along the road. Write the words of the memory verse on the lines at the bottom. In the blanks near the faces, write the names of friends you can talk to about Jesus.

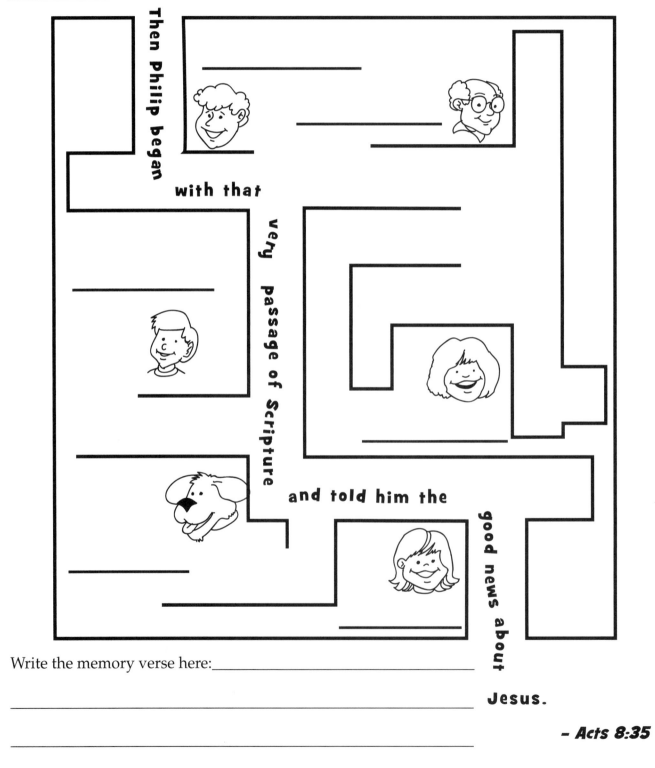

Then Philip began with that very passage of Scripture and told him the good news about Jesus.

Write the memory verse here: _____

_____

_____

— *Acts 8:35*

The solution is on page 96.

Dorcas Helps the Widows
ACTS 9:36-42

✓ MEMORY VERSE

And do not forget to do good and to share with others, for with such sacrifices God is pleased.
~ Hebrews 13:16

WHAT YOU NEED

- page 48, duplicated
- page 48, duplicated on card stock
- markers

BEFORE CLASS

Duplicate a pattern page for each child. Duplicate a second copy for each child on card stock. Make a sample craft to show the children.

WHAT TO DO

1. Introduce the lesson by telling the story from Acts 9:36-42. Ask, **What did Dorcas do for the widows? Why do you think Dorcas did this? How can we do good for older people?**
2. Show the sample craft to the children.
3. Distribute the two copies of the pattern page to each child. Read the memory verse together.
4. Have children cut the figure of the woman out of the card stock. Direct them to use markers to color the robes on the copy paper. Each robe should be colored differently to show different clothes. Have them cut out the robes and dress the paper doll.
5. Repeat the memory verse. Ask, **What kind, good things can we do for older ladies who don't have husbands?** Have children write their ideas on the backs of the robes.

EXTRA TIME

Have the children decorate white handkerchiefs, using fabric pens to draw a heart or a cross in the corner. Plan to distribute the handkerchiefs to widows/widowers in your church, as well as elderly people living alone, or residents at a nursing home.

Dorcas made clothes for widows in her church. Make several robes for this widow. What good things can you do for an older person in the church?

And do not forget to do good and to share with others, for with such sacrifices God is pleased.

– Hebrews 13:16

Peter Learns the Good News is For Everyone
ACTS 10:9-35

✓ MEMORY VERSE

Then Peter began to speak: "I now realize how true it is that God does not show favoritism but accepts men from every nation who fear him and do what is right."
~ Acts 10:34, 35

WHAT YOU NEED

- page 50, duplicated
- pencils

BEFORE CLASS

Duplicate a pattern page for each child.

WHAT TO DO

1. Introduce the lesson by telling the story from Acts 10:9-35. Say, **Peter and the other Jews thought Jesus came to save only the Jews. They didn't think the Good News about what Jesus did on the cross was for other people too. God wants everyone to know about Jesus, even people who are very different from you and me.**
2. Distribute a pattern page to each child.
3. Say the memory verse.
4. Ask the children to name someone they know who is very different from them: ethnically, socially, or in age. Have them write that person's name in the blanks and complete the rest of the page. Ask, **Would it be hard for you to tell this person about Jesus? Why?** Say, **It takes courage to talk about Jesus, especially to people we aren't used to talking to. You can ask God to help you have courage.**

EXTRA TIME

Have children make a collage of faces from magazine and newspaper photos of different faces. Have them glue the faces to a piece of poster board. Title the poster, "Good News Is For Everyone."

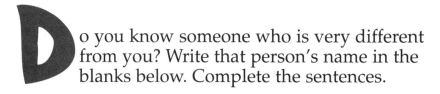

o you know someone who is very different from you? Write that person's name in the blanks below. Complete the sentences.

GOOD NEWS FOR WHO?

_____ is different from me because _____

_____.

_____ needs to know about Jesus.

I can tell _____ about Jesus by (circle at least two ideas below):

    1. Sharing about something Jesus did for me.

    2. Inviting _____ to go to church with me.

    3. Saying I will pray for _____.

    4. Telling _____ how to become a Christian.

    5. Do kind things for _____ that Jesus would like me to do.

Another way I can share the good news is by

_____.

Then Peter began to speak: "I now realize how true it is that God does not show favoritism but accepts men from every nation who fear him and do what is right."
– Acts 10:34, 35

Barnabas and Paul Become Missionaries
ACTS 13:1-5, 13-15, 48-49

✓MEMORY VERSE

Therefore go and make disciples of all nations, baptizing them in the name of the Father and of the Son and of the Holy Spirit and teaching them to obey everything I have commanded you.
~ Matthew 28:19, 20

WHAT YOU NEED

- page 52, duplicated on card stock
- Bibles
- scissors
- yarn, cut in 3 foot lengths
- hole punch

BEFORE CLASS

Duplicate a pattern page for each child. Make a sample craft to show the children.

WHAT TO DO

1. Introduce the lesson by telling the story from Acts 13:1-5, 13-15, 48,49. Say, **God had a special job for Paul and Barnabas. He wanted them to travel to other cities to tell people about Jesus.**
2. Show the sample craft to the children.
3. Distribute a Bible and a pattern page to each child. Help children find Matthew 28:19, 20 in their Bibles. Ask someone to read the verse aloud. Say, **If everyone just stays in their town, people in other countries won't know about Jesus. Some need to go to other countries to tell the good news about Jesus.**
4. Have children cut out and punch holes at the top of each verse segment. Have them string the cards in order, referring to the Bible text as needed. As children finish, have each child read the verse to you.

EXTRA TIME

Use one child's String-a-Verse for this activity. Choose seven children to stand in a line, each holding one of the seven cards. Go down the line, asking each child to read their part of the verse. Say, **It took all of you to complete the verse. It takes all of us to go and help other people become Jesus' followers.**

Make a String-A-Verse to remind yourself that all of us need to pass on the Good News about Jesus to everyone!

Therefore go ◯

and make disciples of all nations, ◯

baptizing them ◯

in the name of the Father and of the Son and of the Holy Spirit ◯

and teaching them to obey ◯

everything I have commanded you. ◯

— Matthew 28:19, 20 ◯

Barnabas and Paul Travel
ACTS 14:1-18

✓ MEMORY VERSE

We are therefore Christ's ambassadors, as though God were making his appeal through us. We implore you on Christ's behalf: Be reconciled to God.
~ 2 Corinthians 5:20

WHAT YOU NEED

- page 54, duplicated
- crayons
- pencils

BEFORE CLASS

Duplicate a pattern page for each child.

WHAT TO DO

1. Ask, **What is a missionary?** Tell the story from Acts 14:1-18. Ask, **Were Paul and Barnabas missionaries? What made them missionaries?** Say, **A missionary is someone who goes to a different country so he or she can tell the people who live there about Jesus.**
2. Distribute a pattern page to each child.
3. Say the memory verse. Explain that an ambassador is someone who travels to another country to help that country be friends with his country. Say, **Paul and Barnabas were ambassadors of Jesus because they wanted people to be friends with God.**
4. Help students locate and circle Antioch, Paul's hometown. Help them locate Iconium and Lystra, the towns where Paul and Barnabas travelled. Ask, **Did the people understand what Paul and Barnabas told them?**
5. Repeat the memory verse. Say, **God wants us to be His ambassadors too.** Help children complete the sentences on the pattern page.

EXTRA TIME

Play the ABC game. Have children take turns saying, "I'm going to tell people about Jesus in... "(name a city, state or country that begins with consecutive letters of the alphabet)."

Circle "Antioch" with a red crayon.
Circle "Iconium" and "Lystra" with a green crayon.
Draw a line from Antioch to Iconium.

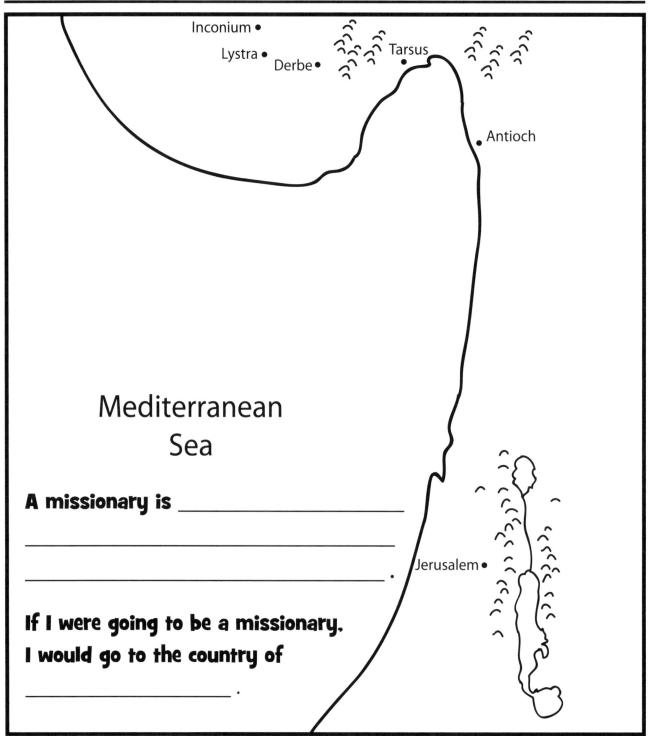

Inconium •

Lystra •

Derbe •

Tarsus

Antioch

Mediterranean
Sea

A missionary is _____
_____
_____ •

Jerusalem •

**If I were going to be a missionary,
I would go to the country of**
_____ •

*We are therefore Christ's ambassadors, as though God were making his appeal through us.
We implore you on Christ's behalf: Be reconciled to God.*
– 2 Corinthians 5:20

54

John Mark Gets Homesick
ACTS 12:25-13:5; 15:36-41

✓ **MEMORY VERSE**

*And surely I am with you always,
to the very end of the age.*
~ Matthew 28:20

WHAT YOU NEED

- page 56, duplicated
- pencils

BEFORE CLASS

Duplicate a pattern page for each child.

WHAT TO DO

1. Introduce the lesson by describing the life of John Mark as told in Acts 12:25-13:5, and 15:36-41. Say, **John Mark was a young man who helped Paul and Barnabas in their mission work. But John Mark became homesick and quit. At first, Paul didn't want John Mark to be his helper anymore but later, Paul realized that John Mark was a good helper for Jesus.**
2. Distribute a pattern page to each child.
3. Say the memory verse.
4. Ask, **Have you ever been homesick? How do you think John Mark felt? What do you think he might have written his mom while he was on his mission trip?** Direct students to complete the post cards.
5. Say, **John Mark gave in to his homesickness once. But he didn't let it stop him from going on another mission trip. Even when we aren't with our families, we can be sure God is with us and will take care of us.**

EXTRA TIME

Let the children share times they've been homesick. Ask each one how they dealt with it. Reassure them homesickness is normal and they can try again. Say, **Missionaries can get homesick because they are just ordinary people like you. When you get homesick, remember that God is always with you and He will take care of you.** Repeat the memory verse.

FIVE MINUTE

How might John Mark have felt when he left his mom to go on a mission trip? On the postcards below, write what you think he might have been thinking during his travels.

ANTIOCH

Dear Mom:
We're in Antioch. We're about to leave for our big mission trip.

_____

_____

Love, John Mark

CYPRUS

Dear Mom:
Now we're in Cyprus. I saw Paul heal a man.

_____

_____

PERGA

Dear Mom:
We left Cyprus. Now we're in Perga.

_____

_____

Love, John Mark

JERUSALEM

Dear Barnabas:
I'm now home in Jerusalem. I can understand why Paul is upset with me.

_____

Can I go with you again sometime?

Your friend, John Mark

And surely I am with you always, to the very end of the age.
– Matthew 28:20

Paul Makes Timothy His Helper
ACTS 16:1-5, 19:21,22

✓ MEMORY VERSE

And the things you have heard me say in the presence of many witnesses entrust to reliable men who will also be qualified to teach others.
~ 2 Timothy 2:2

WHAT YOU NEED

- page 58, duplicated
- pencils

BEFORE CLASS

Duplicate a pattern page for each child.

WHAT TO DO

1. Introduce the lesson by telling the story from Acts 16:1-5; 19:21,22. (Leave out the part about Paul circumcising Timothy.) Say, **Paul took Timothy on his mission trip to be his helper. After awhile, Paul sent Timothy to work in one city while Paul stayed in another city to finish his work. That way, they were able to tell twice as many people about Jesus.**
2. Distribute a pattern page to each child.
3. Say the memory verse.
4. Have students complete the math problems. Have older students help younger students as the numbers become bigger. Say, **If each of us tells somebody about Jesus, then both of you tell two other people about Jesus, we'll be able to tell the world about Jesus a lot faster!**

EXTRA TIME

Print the memory verse on index cards, enough for one per child. Place them in a stack at one end of your room. Ask one child to distribute the cards to all the children, running to get one at a time. Ask, **Is there a better way to pass out these cards?** Brainstorm. Suggest the child get helpers. Say, **We'll get the word out about Jesus faster if we teach other people how to tell about Jesus, too.**

 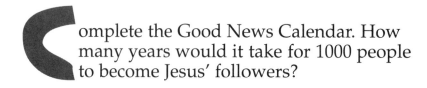

omplete the Good News Calendar. How many years would it take for 1000 people to become Jesus' followers?

Good News Calendar

Year One: You tell someone about Jesus. 1 + 1 = _____

Year Two: Both of you tell two others about Jesus. 2 + 2 = _____

Year Three: _____ of you tell _____ others about Jesus. 4 + 4 = _____

Year Four: _____ + _____ = _____
Year ____: _____ + _____ = _____
Year ____: _____ + _____ = _____
Year ____: _____ + _____ = _____
Year ____: _____ + _____ = _____
Year ____: _____ + _____ = _____
Year ____: _____ + _____ = _____

How many years will it take to tell 1000 people about Jesus? _____

And the things you have heard me say in the presence of many witnesses entrust to reliable men who will also be qualified to teach others.
– 2 Timothy 2:2

The solution is on page 96.

Lydia Helps Paul and Silas
ACTS 16:11-15, 40

✓ MEMORY VERSE

Share with God's people who are in need.
Practice hospitality.
~ Romans 12:13

WHAT YOU NEED

- page 60, duplicated
- colored pencils or markers

BEFORE CLASS

Duplicate a pattern page for each child.

WHAT TO DO

1. Introduce the lesson by telling the story from Acts 16: 11-15, 40. Ask, **What did Lydia invite Paul to do?** Say, **Paul and his traveling friends needed a place to stay. Lydia helped them in their mission work by letting them stay at her house. We can help God's special workers too.**
2. Distribute a pattern page to each child.
3. Say the memory verse. Explain that hospitality means being friendly and helpful to guests and strangers.
4. Tell students to draw a picture of how Lydia used her house for Jesus. Brainstorm ways they and their families can use their house for Jesus, such as inviting Christian workers for a meal, providing a place to stay overnight, baking cookies for a sick neighbor, or having a party for the youth group. Ask the children to draw one of the ideas in the second house.

EXTRA TIME

Provide a snack and have children enjoy the snack sitting at a table. Have one child pretend to be a visiting missionary from a country of their choice. Ask the rest of the group to ask the "missionary" questions about his work. Say, **When we invite God's special workers to our church or home, we can learn a lot of things about the work they do, the people they work with, and the place where they live.**

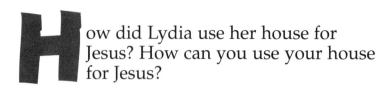

How did Lydia use her house for Jesus? How can you use your house for Jesus?

Share with God's people who are in need. Practice hospitality.
– Romans 12:13

The Bereans Check the Bible
ACTS 17:1-12

✓ **MEMORY VERSE**

All Scripture is God-breathed and is useful for teaching, rebuking, correcting and training in righteousness.
~ 2 Timothy 3:16

WHAT YOU NEED

- page 62, duplicated
- pencils

BEFORE CLASS

Duplicate a pattern page for each child.

WHAT TO DO

1. Introduce the lesson by telling the story from Acts 17:1-12. Say, **People reacted in different ways when they heard about Jesus. Some people became angry. They thought Paul was doing a bad thing. But the people in Berea checked the Old Testament to see if what he was saying was true. Guess what? It was true! The Bible predicted that Jesus would come and die, then come back to life. So they became Christians.**
2. Distribute a pattern page to each child.
3. Say the memory verse.
4. Have the children use the memory verse to unscramble the words. Say, **Everything in the Bible is true! You can use what the Bible says to live life God's way. The Bible helps us know the right way to live (this is called teaching), where you went wrong (this is called rebuking), how to start living right again (this is called correcting) and how to keep on doing right (this is called training in righteousness).** Have the children move their finger to each point as you speak. **The Bible is a great book!**

EXTRA TIME

Have your group work together to create a TV or radio commercial that promotes the Bible. Use a digital camcorder or voice recorder to tape their commercial then play it back for the class.

The Bible is like a GPS guidance system. God's word will guide you to where you need to be. Use the memory verse below to unscramble the words.

GPS

Destination: Heaven!

The right way to go:

___ ___ ___ ___ ___ ___ ___ ___ ___ (cahegint)

When we go in the wrong direction:

___ ___ ___ ___ ___ ___ ___ ___ (grenbuik)

How to start doing right:

___ ___ ___ ___ ___ ___ ___ ___ ___ ___ (rccentgior)

And how to stay on the right road:

___ ___ ___ ___ ___ ___ ___ ___ **in righteousness** (rtianngi)

All Scripture is God-breathed and is useful for teaching, rebuking, correcting and training in righteousness.
- 2 Timothy 3:16

The solution is on page 96.

Priscilla, Aquila, and Apollos
ACTS 18:1-4, 24-28

✓ MEMORY VERSE

Be completely humble and gentle; be patient,
bearing with one another in love.
~ Ephesians 4:2

WHAT YOU NEED

- page 64, duplicated
- crayons
- transparent tape

BEFORE CLASS

Duplicate a pattern page for each child. Make a sample craft to show the children.

WHAT TO DO

1. Introduce the lesson by telling the story from Acts 18:1-4, 24-28. Say, **Apollos wasn't teaching the right facts about Jesus. Aquila and Priscilla could have argued with him in front of everyone.** Ask, **What did they do instead?**
2. Show the sample craft to the children.
3. Say the memory verse.
4. Have the children color the pictures then fold the page on the fold lines, so the page forms a triangle. Tape the ends.
5. Say, **When someone is wrong, it's OK to let them know they are wrong. But it's important to do it in a nice way that doesn't embarrass them or hurt their feelings.** Ask, **What are some other nice ways to tell people they are wrong?** Repeat the memory verse together.

EXTRA TIME

Role play practicing right ways and wrong ways to correct people who have their facts mixed up. Use these starters: "Man evolved from toads," "You don't have to believe in Jesus in order to go to heaven," "There really are monsters from Mars," or use your own false facts to start the role play. Repeat the memory verse. Ask, **How can you show patience and gentleness with people who have their facts mixed up?**

Make a folding scene to tell the story about Priscilla, Aquila, and Apollos. Color the pictures.

Be completely humble and gentle; be patient, bearing with one another in love.
– Ephesians 4:2

Paul Says Goodbye to His Friends
ACTS 20:13-38

✓ MEMORY VERSE

In everything I did, I showed you that by this kind of hard work we must help the weak, remembering the words the Lord Jesus himself said, "It is more blessed to give than to receive."
~ Acts 20:35

WHAT YOU NEED

- page 66, duplicated
- markers

BEFORE CLASS

Duplicate a pattern page for each child. Make a sample craft to show the children.

WHAT TO DO

1. Ask, **If you were going to never see a good friend again, what would you want to say to your friend?** Tell the story from Acts 20:13-38. Say, **Paul had been a preacher in Ephesus for three years. These men were his good friends. He knew he would never see them again, so he said what was most important to him. He wanted them to take good care of the church and to always be faithful to God.**
2. Show the sample craft to the children.
3. Distribute a pattern page to each child.
4. Say the memory verse. Have the children repeat it with you.
5. Have the children use markers to color in the words of the verse and to decorate the outer edges to make a verse poster. Say, **These words are the last words Paul said to his friends in Ephesus.** Ask, **What was the important message Paul wanted his friends to remember? How can we follow Paul's advice?**

EXTRA TIME

Provide materials for the children to add a frame to their picture. Help them cut out a one inch frame from card stock or poster board to glue on top of the verse picture, then decorate the frame with fabric, drawings or other art material.

Make a verse poster of this important advice from the Apostle Paul.

In everything I did, I showed you that by this kind of hard work we must help the weak, remembering the words the Lord Jesus himself said, "It is more blessed to give than to receive."
– Acts 20:35

Paul's Nephew Uncovers a Plot
ACTS 23:12-24

✓ MEMORY VERSE

Don't let anyone look down on you because you are young, but set an example for the believers in speech, in life, in love, in faith and in purity.
~ 1 Timothy 4:12

WHAT YOU NEED

- page 68, duplicated
- pencils

BEFORE CLASS

Duplicate a pattern page for each child.

WHAT TO DO

1. Introduce the lesson by reading this exciting story from Acts 23:12-24. Say, **We don't know how old Paul's nephew was, but he was probably your age. God used this boy to keep Paul safe. God can use you, too. God loves to use ordinary people, even kids, to do His work.**
2. Distribute a pattern page to each child.
3. Say the memory verse.
4. Say, **God uses ordinary people, even children, to do His work!** Ask, **What kind of things would you like to do for God?** Brainstorm ideas with your group, then ask each person to write their dreams on the pattern page.
5. Repeat the verse together. Say, **You can start right now to live the way God wants you to. When you do, God can do great things through you no matter how old or young you are.**

EXTRA TIME

Ask your group what other Bible stories tell about children whom God used to do His work. If children can't remember, guide their thinking by mentioning David and Goliath, the boy who shared his lunch with Jesus, Samuel, and Josiah. If children remember the story line, have them act out the story for the others to guess.

What big thing would you like to do for God? He'll help you do it! Write it here.

Don't let anyone look down on you because you are young, but set an example for the believers in speech, in life, in love, in faith and in purity.
– 1 Timothy 4:12

The Christians Encourage Paul in Rome
ACTS 28:11-16

✓MEMORY VERSE

An anxious heart weighs a man down,
but a kind word cheers him up.
~ Proverbs 12:25.

WHAT YOU NEED

- page 70, duplicated on pink paper
- scissors
- glue
- pencils
- red construction paper

BEFORE CLASS

Duplicate a pattern page for each child. Make a sample craft to show the children.

WHAT TO DO

1. Introduce the lesson by telling the story from Acts 28:11-16. Say, **Paul was a prisoner. He had just finished a very rough sea voyage.** Ask, **How do you think Paul felt when he got to Rome? What encouraged Paul? Why would that be encouraging to Paul?**
2. Show the sample craft to the children.
3. Distribute a pattern page to each child.
4. Say the memory verse.
5. Have children write four different, nice things they could say to friends such as, "Good job," "You're a great friend," or "Keep up the good work."
6. Have them cut out the hearts and exchange them with four other children.
7. Have the children make a place mat by cutting out the large heart, gluing it in the center of the construction paper, then gluing the smaller hearts around the larger heart. Say, **Sometimes being a Christian is tough. God gives us our Christian friends in His church to encourage us and to help us remember we are not alone.**

EXTRA TIME

Teach the children the words to the hymn, "We Are One In The Bond Of Love" or another song about the church or friendship. Repeat the memory verse together.

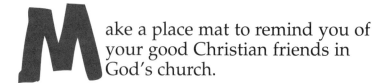ake a place mat to remind you of your good Christian friends in God's church.

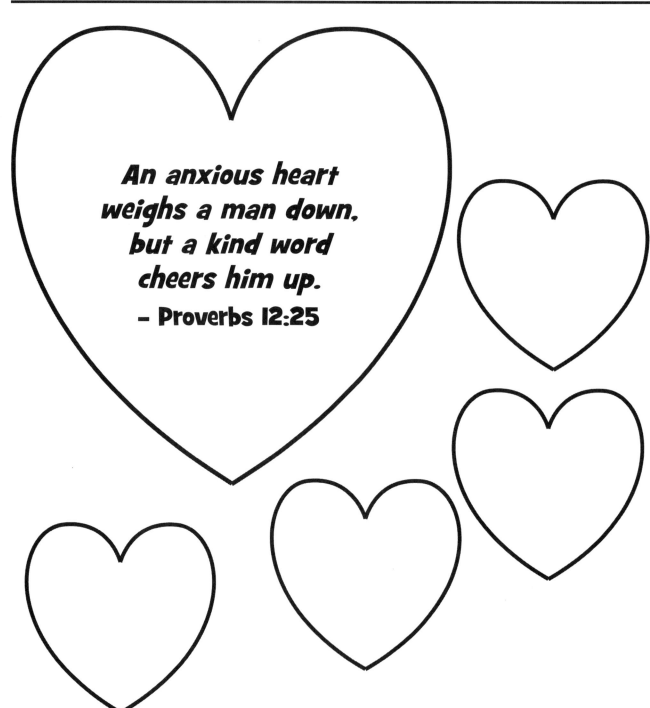

An anxious heart weighs a man down, but a kind word cheers him up.

– Proverbs 12:25

Saul Meets Jesus
ACTS 9:1-19

✓ MEMORY VERSE

But the Lord said to Ananias, "Go. This man is my chosen instrument to carry my name before... the people of Israel."
~ Acts 9:15

WHAT YOU NEED

- page 72, duplicated
- colored copy paper
- pencils
- scissors
- paper fasteners
- crayons

BEFORE CLASS

Duplicate a pattern page for each child. Make a sample craft to show the children.

WHAT TO DO

1. Introduce the lesson by telling the story from Acts 9:1-19. Ask, **Why was Saul going to Damascus? Who did Saul meet? What did Jesus tell Saul to do?**
2. Show the sample craft to the children. Say, **Saul used to punish and kill people because they were Christians. Jesus showed Saul He was real so Saul could do a special job for God.**
3. Distribute a pattern page to each child. Say the memory verse. Ask, **What special job did God have for Saul?** Explain that a Gentile was someone in another country who didn't even believe in God and definitely knew nothing about Jesus.
4. Tell the children to cut out the job wheel and draw two more jobs they would like to have in the blank spaces. Have them trace around the wheel on a blank sheet of paper, then cut out the circle. Have them mark the center, cut out a pie shaped section from the blank circle, then attach the two circles, the blank piece on top, with a paper fastener. Color the scenes as time allows. Say, **God called Saul to go tell people in other countries about Jesus. Someday, God might call you to do a special job for Him.**

EXTRA TIME

Say, **Saul first needed to believe in Jesus before he could do God's special job.**
Ask one of your church leaders to visit your class to explain what someone needs to do to become a Christian.

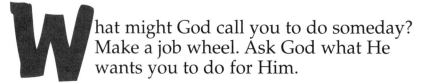

What might God call you to do someday? Make a job wheel. Ask God what He wants you to do for Him.

But the Lord said to Ananias, "Go. This man is my chosen instrument to carry my name before the Gentiles and their kings and before the people of Israel."
– Acts 9:15

Saul's Escape
ACTS 9:19-25

✓ **MEMORY VERSE**

You are my hiding place; You will protect me from trouble and surround me with songs of deliverance.
~ Psalm 32:7

WHAT YOU NEED

- page 74, duplicated
- scissors
- pencils

BEFORE CLASS

Duplicate a pattern page for each child. Make a sample craft to show the children.

WHAT TO DO

1. Introduce the lesson by telling the story from Acts 9:19-25. Ask, **What did Saul do after he became a Christian? Why did his friends need to help him escape? Why do you think some people wouldn't like him to talk about Jesus?**
2. Show the sample craft to the children.
3. Distribute a pattern page to each child.
4. Read the memory verse together. Say, **God protected Saul from the people who wanted to kill him because God had an important job for Saul to do.**
5. Ask children to draw themselves inside Jesus' arms. Have them write how someone might react if they didn't want to hear a Christian talk about Jesus. Have the children cut out the figure and show them how to fold the arms on the fold lines so they cross over their drawing. Say, **When you talk about Jesus or live like a Christian, God will protect you so you can keep talking about Jesus.**

EXTRA TIME

Write the following countries on slips of paper and place in a basket: India, China, Indonesia, Sudan, Iran. Have students each select a slip and lead them in praying for persecuted Christians in those countries. For specific information on persecuted Christians check the website "Voice of the Martyrs," (www.persecution.com). Say, **We pray that God will protect His people when they stand up for their beliefs.**

FIVE MINUTE

Write what someone could do to you if they didn't like you talking about Jesus. Fold Jesus' arms over you. He will protect you!

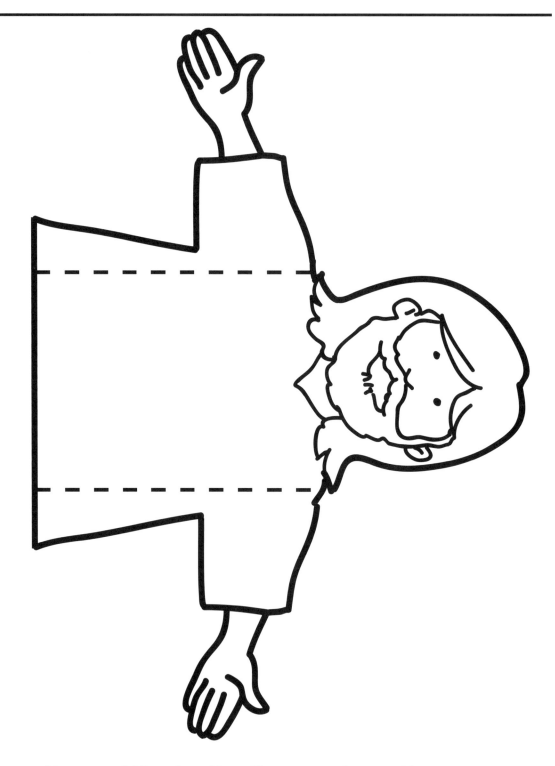

*You are my hiding place; You will protect me from trouble
and surround me with songs of deliverance.*
– Psalm 32:7

Cornelius Learns About Jesus
ACTS 10:1-8, 23-48

✓ MEMORY VERSE

All the prophets testify about him that everyone who believes in him receives forgiveness of sins through his name.
~ Acts 10:43

WHAT YOU NEED

- page 76, duplicated
- legal sized paper
- scissors
- tape
- yarn
- hole punch

BEFORE CLASS

Duplicate a pattern page for each child. Make a sample craft to show the children.

WHAT TO DO

1. Introduce the lesson by telling the story from Acts 10:1-8, 23-48. Ask, **How did Cornelius show his faith in God? What did the angel tell Cornelius to do? When Cornelius heard about Jesus, what happened?**
2. Show the sample craft to the children.
3. Distribute a pattern page to each child.
4. Say the memory verse. Say, **This is the message God wants people to hear.** Ask, **How do people find out this message?**
5. Have students color and cut out the four figures then punch holes at the top of each figure, tying a loop of yarn through each hole. Have them thread a longer piece of yarn through the loops like a clothesline in this order: angel, Cornelius, messengers, Peter. Have them tape each end of the yarn to the legal sized paper, leaving a little slack in the yarn so the figures can move.
6. Show students how to tell the story by moving the figures back and forth. Say, **Peter told Cornelius about Jesus who became a Christian. The church gets bigger when more and more people learn about Jesus and become Christians like Cornelius.**

EXTRA TIME

Ask, **How do people who don't know about Jesus find out about Jesus?** Have your group make a poster that tells about Jesus.

Make a story line about Cornelius. Move your figures along the yarn line to tell the story.

Messengers

Peter

Cornelius

Angel

All the prophets testify about him that everyone who believes in him receives forgiveness of sins through his name.
– Acts 10:43

God Tells Paul to Go to Macedonia
ACTS 16:6-12

✓ MEMORY VERSE

*In all your ways acknowledge Him,
and He will make your paths straight.*
~ Proverbs 3:6

WHAT YOU NEED

- page 78, duplicated on card stock
- pencils
- crayons
- scissors
- tape

BEFORE CLASS

Duplicate a pattern page for each child. Make a sample craft to show the children.

WHAT TO DO

1. Introduce the lesson by telling the story from Acts 16:6-12. Say, **God REALLY wants His church to grow. He wants people to believe in Jesus and become part of the church. Because God wants the church to grow, He will help you know who you should talk to about Jesus.**
2. Show the sample craft to the children.
3. Distribute a pattern page to each child.
4. Say the memory verse. Say, **If you are trying to obey Jesus, He will help you know what to do, including who you can talk to about Jesus.**
5. Have children cut out the bookmark. On the back side, have them write the name of someone they know who isn't a Christian. Have them color and decorate the bookmarks, fold in half, then tape the sides together. Lead the group in praying for opportunities to tell the people they have written on the inside of their bookmarks about Jesus.

EXTRA TIME

Play a variation of "Mother May I?" Students take turns asking to go various places in the room. The leader will answer, "Yes you may" or, "No you may not" and give another place to go. Students try to move so they work their way toward the leader.

ake a bookmark. Ask God to help you know what you can do for Him.

And He will make your paths straight.

In all your ways acknowledge Him...

Paul Tells a Jail Guard About Jesus
ACTS 16:22-34

✓ MEMORY VERSE

Believe on the Lord Jesus and you will be saved.
~ Acts 16:31

WHAT YOU NEED

- page 80, duplicated
- pencils
- crayons

BEFORE CLASS

Duplicate a pattern page for each child.

WHAT TO DO

1. Introduce the lesson by telling the story from Acts 16:22-34. Say, **Paul and Silas were in jail because they told people about Jesus. God rescued them by sending an earthquake to break the doors of the jail. The jailer thought the prisoners had escaped and he would be in trouble. Paul used this chance to tell him about Jesus.**
2. Distribute a pattern page to each child.
3. Say the memory verse. Say, **The jailer asked what he could do to be saved. What did Paul and Silas tell him?** Have the children repeat the memory verse with you.
4. Discuss each of the situations shown on the pattern page. Say, **Each of these situations is a chance to tell someone about Jesus. How could you tell these people about Jesus?** Have students give ideas, then have the children write in answers. When they have finished, discuss other times when children might be able to talk about Jesus to other people, then have students draw a cartoon of their ideas in the blank space. As time allows, let children color the pictures.

EXTRA TIME

Have the children take turns role playing one of the provided situations or another one they have created.

How would you tell the people below about Jesus? Write what you could say in the speech bubbles. In the blank space, draw another way we can talk to others about Jesus.

Believe on the Lord Jesus and you will be saved.
– Acts 16:31

God Comforts Paul in a Dream
ACTS 18:5-11

✓ **MEMORY VERSE**

*Do not be afraid, keep on speaking,
do not be silent.*
~ Acts 18:9

WHAT YOU NEED

- page 82, duplicated
- scissors
- lunch size paper bags
- glue
- markers

BEFORE CLASS

Duplicate a pattern page for each child. Make a sample craft to show the children.

WHAT TO DO

1. Introduce the lesson by telling the story from Acts 18:5-11. Ask, **Who didn't want Paul to talk about Jesus? When Paul kept talking about Jesus, who became a Christian? How did God encourage Paul to keep talking about Jesus?**
2. Show the sample craft to the children.
3. Distribute a pattern page to each child. Say the memory verse. Say, **God encouraged Paul in a dream to keep telling people about Jesus. He reminded Paul that He would always be with Paul.**
4. Have the children cut out the verse strips and glue them to the front of the paper bag, below the fold. Have them draw a picture of their face above and below the fold so they make a puppet of themselves.
5. Tell the children to repeat the memory verse, saying it as they move the "mouth" of their paper bag puppet.

EXTRA TIME

Brainstorm facts about Jesus children can tell others such as "Jesus died for you," "God is always with you," "Jesus can take care of you" or "God forgives you when you do wrong things." Have the children say the sentences using their paper bag puppets.

Make a puppet to remind yourself not to be afraid to talk about Jesus.

Do not be afraid.

Keep on speaking.

Do not be silent.
– Acts 18:9

Do not be afraid, keep on speaking, do not be silent.
– Acts 18:9

Christians Get Rid of Bad Stuff
ACTS 19:17-20

✓ MEMORY VERSE

But now you must rid yourselves of all such things as these: anger, rage, malice, slander, and filthy language from your lips.
~ Colossians 3:8

WHAT YOU NEED

- page 84, duplicated
- Bibles
- pencils
- white acrylic paint
- paintbrushes
- water

BEFORE CLASS

Duplicate a pattern page for each child. Make a sample craft to show the children.

WHAT TO DO

1. Introduce the lesson by telling the story from Acts 19:17-20. Say, **The Christians at Ephesus wanted to please God so much, they were willing to get rid of things that would keep them from following God. God also wants us to get rid of things that will keep us from following Him, like bad habits and bad behaviors.**
2. Distribute a pattern page and a Bible to each child. Help the children find Colossians 3:8. Have an older reader read the verse out loud.
3. Have the children use their Bibles and the words inside the boy to complete the verse on the pattern page. Define the different words for the children in simple ways they can understand.
4. Say, **God wants us to act like we are following Him. When we act like everyone else acts, other people won't be able to tell that we are Jesus' followers.** Have the children paint over the words inside the child.

EXTRA TIME

Have children write on a piece of paper a behavior they do that is not pleasing to God, like filthy language, getting angry at parents or siblings, or talking nasty about other children. Say, **God wants us to get rid of these behaviors. He can help us.** Lead the children in wadding up the paper and throwing it in the trash can.

What does God want you to get rid of? Use the words written on the child to complete the memory verse. Cross out the words once you have written them in the verse.

anger

filthy

language

malice

rage

slander

But now you must rid yourselves of all such things as these: __ __ __ __ __ ,

__ __ __ __ , __ __ __ __ __ __ __ , __ __ __ __ __ __ __ , and

__ __ __ __ __ __ __ __ __ __ __ __ __ __ **from your lips.**

– Colossians 3:8

The solution is on page 96.

Eutychus Falls Out the Window
ACTS 20:7-12

✓ MEMORY VERSE

On the first day of the week we came together to break bread. Paul spoke to the people and, because he intended to leave the next day, kept on talking until midnight.
~ Acts 20:7

WHAT YOU NEED

- page 86, duplicated
- pencils
- scissors
- hole punch
- yarn

BEFORE CLASS

Duplicate a pattern page for each child. Make a sample craft to show the children. Write on your plaque why the church is personally special to you.

WHAT TO DO

1. Ask, **Have you ever become sleepy from sitting too long in a warm room?** Introduce the lesson by telling the story from Acts 20:7-12. Say, **The church in Ephesus must have been excited that Paul was coming to visit them. The church people wanted to hear Paul speak, even if it meant staying at church for hours! Poor Eutychus fell asleep in the warm, stuffy room and fell from the third story. But God's power brought him back to life.**
2. Show the sample craft to the children. Read what you have written on your plaque.
3. Distribute a pattern page to each child. Read the memory verse. Ask, **What is the first day of the week?**
4. Ask, **What is special about our church? Why do you like to come to church?** Ask children to write about the church on the wall plaque. Help those who have difficulty writing. When done, have the children cut out the wall plaque and thread a piece of yarn through the top to make a wall hanging.

EXTRA TIME

Provide a snack of grape juice and crackers for the children. Explain that the early church liked to get together to eat a meal that helped them remember how Jesus died for their sins.

Five Minute

What is special about your church? Tell about your church below. Make a wall plaque to remind you about your special church.

On the first day of the week we came together to break bread. Paul spoke to the people and, because he intended to leave the next day, kept on talking until midnight.

– Acts 20:7

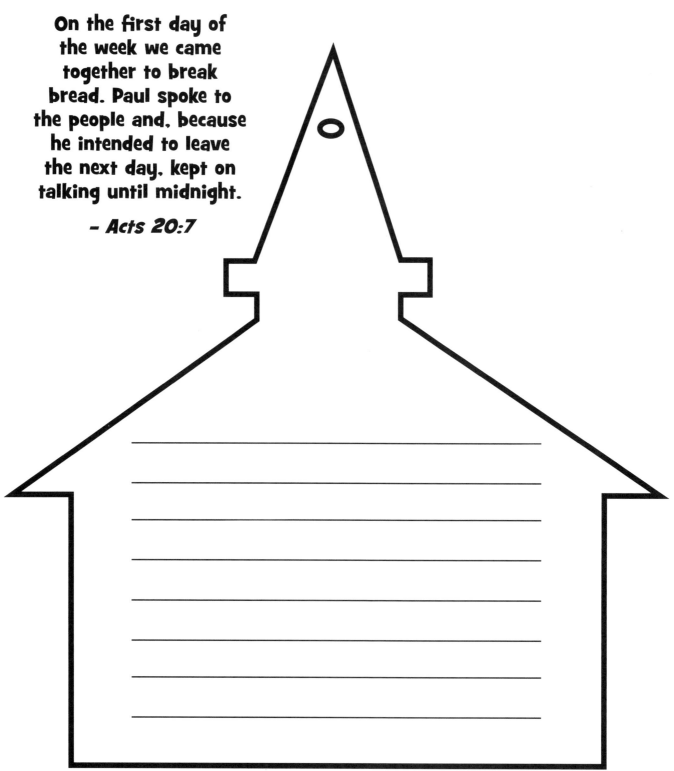

Paul Tells a King About Jesus
ACTS 25:13-26:31

✓ MEMORY VERSE

Always be prepared to give an answer to everyone who asks you to give the reason for the hope that you have. But do this with gentleness and respect.
~ 1 Peter 3:15

WHAT YOU NEED

- page 88, duplicated
- 11' x 14' pieces of poster board
- scissors
- glue
- pencils
- blank paper

BEFORE CLASS

Duplicate a pattern page for each child. Make a sample newspaper story to show the children.

WHAT TO DO

1. Introduce the lesson by telling the story from Acts 25:13-26:31. Say, **Wow! Paul had the chance to tell a king and a governor how he became a Christian. He almost convinced the king to become a Christian.**
2. Show the sample craft to the children.
3. Distribute a pattern page and a piece of poster board to each child.
4. Say the memory verse. Say, **God wants us to be prepared to tell anyone how we became a Christian. Paul told the king three things: what he was like before he was a Christian, how he became a Christian, and what he was doing now that he was a Christian.**
5. Have the children number each story in sequential order. Then cut out the story fragments and glue them in order on the poster board. Have them add pictures or other stories to the newspaper as you have time.

EXTRA TIME

Work as a group to write a story about someone who has become a Christian. It can be one of the children or someone the children know. They can make up a story if they want. Have them include the three main parts of a personal testimony: what the person was like before becoming a Christian, how the person became a Christian, and what the person is doing now to follow Jesus.

Put Paul's story together into a newspaper article by numbering the articles. Then cut out the pages and put them in order. Share Paul's story with a friend.

The Caesarea News

"One day, I was traveling to Damascus. On the road, I saw a bright light. A voice talked to me. 'Saul, why are you persecuting me?' I said, 'Who are you, Lord?' The voice answered, 'I am Jesus. When you hurt Christians, you hurt me. Now go to Damascus and find out what you are to do.' Wow! Jesus really is the Son of God. I was wrong."

"Before I was a Christian, I was a very good Jew. I obeyed God's laws. But I did not like Christians. I thought Christians were wrong. I didn't believe that Jesus was God's Son. So I hurt the Christians. I got permission from the Jewish leaders to arrest Christians and put them in prison. I even went to other countries to find the Christians so they could be put to death."

Paul the Christian who is in prison for talking about Jesus, spoke to Governor Festus and King Agrippa today. Paul is waiting to go to Rome where he will stand trial for his crimes. No one knows what Paul did wrong. King Agrippa and Governor Festus listened to Paul, hoping to get more information about why the Jews want Paul dead. Here is Paul's story.

"So I became a Christian. I was baptized. I started telling people about Jesus. God gave me the job to tell about Jesus to people in other countries. I told everyone that Jesus died and came back to life so he could forgive all of us for the wrong things we do. Now I'm in prison because I believe in Jesus. You can become a Christian like me, King Agrippa."

Always be prepared to give an answer to everyone who asks you to give the reason for the hope that you have. But do this with gentleness and respect.
– 1 Peter 3:15

The solution is on page 96.

Paul Survives a Shipwreck
ACTS 27

✓ MEMORY VERSE

*But now I urge you to keep up your courage,
because not one of you will be lost;
only the ship will be destroyed.*
~ Acts 27:22

WHAT YOU NEED

- page 90, duplicated
- pencils
- crayons

BEFORE CLASS

Duplicate a pattern page for each child.

WHAT TO DO

1. Introduce the lesson by telling the story from Acts 27. Say, **Paul was a prisoner. The soldiers were taking Paul to Rome to stand trial before the king. Paul knew God wanted him to speak to the King about Jesus so Paul knew God would keep him safe even through a hurricane-like storm.**
2. Distribute a pattern page to each child.
3. Read the memory verse.
4. Explain that children will complete the math story by filling in the numbers from the story. Have the children draw pictures above the words. When everyone is done, have the children take turns reading their math story to you. Say, **Even though the ship was destroyed, no one drowned. Ask, Who kept everyone alive in that storm?**

EXTRA TIME

Have children create a boat picture on a foam sheet using chenille wire, small craft sticks, felt and fabric scraps. Guide them in creating titles for their pictures that expresses God's protection of them such as, "God's Looking Out For Me."

Finish the math story about Paul's shipwreck by using numbers in the box. Each will be used only once. Draw pictures to illustrate your math story.

_____ ship + _____ passengers

+ _____ very bad storm + _____ days

- _____ lifeboat - _____ ship + _____ very

powerful God who keeps His promises + _____ lives lost

= _____ alive passengers.

14	1	276
276	1	1
1	0	1

*But now I urge you to keep up your courage, because not one of you will be lost;
only the ship will be destroyed.*
– Acts 27:22

The solution is on page 96.

Paul and the Poisonous Snake
ACTS 28:1-6

> ## ✓ MEMORY VERSE
>
> *The Lord will keep you from all harm—He will watch over your life.*
> ~ Psalm 121:7

WHAT YOU NEED

- page 92, duplicated
- pencils

BEFORE CLASS

Duplicate a pattern page for each child.

WHAT TO DO

1. Introduce the lesson by telling the story from Acts 28:1-6. Ask, **What usually happens when a poisonous snake bites someone? What happened to Paul? Why didn't Paul die from the snake bite?**
2. Distribute a pattern page to each child.
3. Have students put a finger in the middle of the snake coil. Tell them to follow the coil to find today's verse, writing the words in order on the lines below. Have them answer the question at the bottom of the page.
4. Read the memory verse together. Say, **God has the power to protect us from harm. If He has work for us to do, He will keep us safe so we can do the job He wants us to do. God wants His church to grow so He will take care of His people.**

EXTRA TIME

Take a "snake walk." Have kids join hands and weave around your teaching area. Challenge them to make a snake coil without letting go. Have them say the memory verse as they walk.

Follow the coil of the snake to find the words of the memory verse. Write it on the lines below.

The Lord will keep you from all harm — He will watch over your life. – Psalm 121:7

Write the memory verse:

_____ _____ _____ _____ _____ _____ _____

_____ _ _____ _____ _____ _____ _____ _____.

– Psalm 121:7

When the islanders saw that Paul didn't die from the snake bite, they decided he was a god. Who really kept Paul safe from the snake bite? _____

The solution is on page 96.

Paul Preaches in a Prison
ACTS 28:17-31

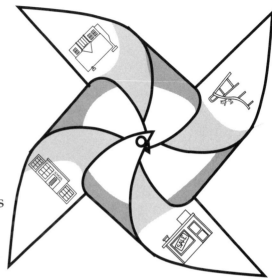

✓ MEMORY VERSE

Boldly and without hindrance he preached the kingdom of God and taught about the Lord Jesus Christ.
~ Acts 28:31

WHAT YOU NEED

- page 94, duplicated
- crayons
- scissors
- paper fasteners
- paper plates
- plastic straws

BEFORE CLASS

Duplicate a pattern page for each child. Make a sample craft to show the children.

WHAT TO DO

1. Tell the story from Acts 28:17-31. Say, **When Paul was put in prison he could have thought that he wouldn't be able to preach about Jesus. But Paul didn't let a prison stop him! Anytime someone came to see Paul, he talked about Jesus!**
2. Show the sample craft to the children.
3. Distribute a pattern page to each child. Say the memory verse.
4. Have children color the pictures, cut out the pinwheel and cut inward on the solid lines
5. Show how to fold every other point to the center dot. Help children attach a paper fastener through all the points through the center of the pinwheel and through the center of a paper plate on the other side. Ask, **How could you talk about Jesus at each of these places?**

EXTRA TIME

Have children name someone they know who needs to know about Jesus in each of the locations on their pinwheel. Have them write the name of that person below the picture. Pray with the children that God will give them a chance to talk about Jesus to their friends this week.

Paul talked about Jesus when he was in prison. Make a pinwheel to show where you can talk about Jesus.

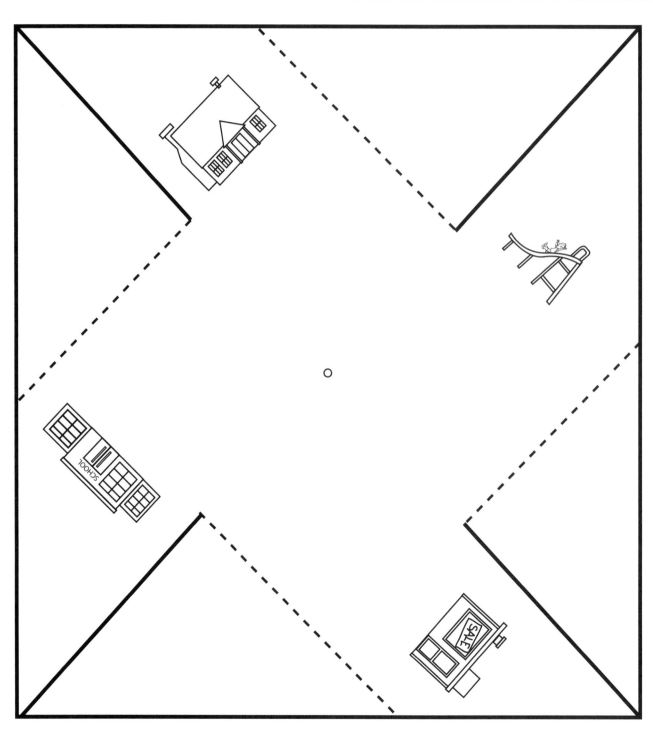

*Boldly and without hindrance he preached the kingdom of God
and taught about the Lord Jesus Christ.*
– Acts 28:31

Puzzle Answers

Page 12

PETER

ANDREW

JAMES

JOHN

PHILLIP

BARTHOLOMEW

THOMAS

MATTHEW

THADDAEUS

SIMON

JAMES ALPHAEUS

JUDAS

Page 14

Chief Priest: "Are you the Christ, the Son of the Blessed One?"
Jesus: "I am."

Page 16

Page 24

What did Peter invite the other disciples to do? (**Come fishing with him**)
When did the disciples go fishing? (**Night**)
How many fish did they catch during the night? (**Zero**)
What did Jesus tell them to do? (**Go fish**)
How many fish did they catch when Jesus told them to fish? (**153**)
What was Jesus doing on the lake shore? (**Making breakfast**)

Page 32

1. People listening to others tell about Jesus.
2. People eating.
3. Sharing with those in need.
4. People singing songs of praise for Jesus.
5. A group of people talking about Jesus.
6. Giving to the poor.

Page 36

They shared everything they had.
– Acts 4:32

Page 38

Do not lie to each other, since you have taken off your old self with its practices.
– Colossians 3:9

Page 46
Then Philip began with that very passage of Scripture and told him the good news about Jesus.
– Acts 8:35

Page 58
Ten

Page 62
Teaching, rebuking, correcting, training

Page 84
*But now you must also rid yourselves of all such things as these: **anger, rage, malice, slander,** and **filthy language** from your lips.*
– Colossians 3:8

Page 88

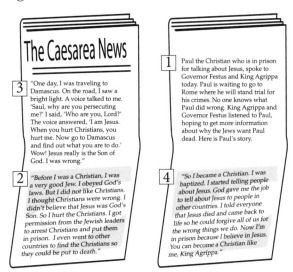

Page 90
1 ship + 276 passengers
+ 1 very bad storm + 14 days
– 1 lifeboat – 1 ship + 1 very powerful God
who keeps His promises + 0 lives lost
= 276 alive passengers.

Page 92
The Lord will keep you from all harm—He will watch over your life.
– Psalm 121:7

Who really kept Paul safe from the snake bite? **God.**